Poems Sublime

by Younas Rehman

INDIA • SINGAPORE • MALAYSIA

ISBN 979-8-89556-991-7

Dedication

The book along with this poem are dedicated to
Younas Rehman by Sunita Grover Raina

Poems Sublime

If I could have
your magical quill

What lovely poems
I could have spilled

Though I too write
and place my thoughts

When read your poems
to heaven brought

A craving wish
takes birth within

To write like you,
poems look a twin

I feel like stealing
all your poesies

Tie them tightly,
use them as rosaries

You are a poet
who speaks 'HIS' words

Your soul I read,
my soul you stirred

If I was got here
to rhyme and chime

It was also to read
your poems sublime.

India

Credits

Sunita Grover Raina for compiling, editing, publishing and designing the covers of the book.
The picture on the front cover is the poet (Younas Rehman) when young.

Poems Sublime

Contents

Foreword

by Dr Jaysankar Basu

Associate Professor and Globally Published Author, attached with the Centre for Language, Translation & Cultural Studies, SoH. NSOU, SoH & CLTCS, NSOU.

To write the foreword to a book of poems by Younas Rehman, the bilingual poet from Pakistan writing in English and Pashto, is indeed a pleasing honour bestowed upon me by Sunita Grover Raina, herself a poet *per se* and the editor of this debut publication of Younas's poetry in English.

Without beating about the bush, let me come straight to the essence and aura of Younas's poetry. I quote from the opening section of the first poem in this collection:

Eventually
I should draw a picture of mine
That refutes the prints of decline
Upon my visage

What a poignant poise and dignity is this in the poet's confession that he is going to unveil a picture of himself – a picture that refutes *the prints of decline / Upon my visage.*

It at once links Younas to the centrepiece of the mosaic of romantic poetry taken out in a timeless numinous zone and out of the effete fetters and labels of chronology or history. More importantly, it places Younas at the heart of the archetypal romantic motif that the self is the centre of the universe, and the poet can do no better than make his own self the subject of creativity. He writes in a form that proceeds from within, in outright rejection of a shape superinduced by cerebral activity. Of course, the poet's creative self is not a disembodied entity, but a constantly perceiving and evolving consciousness via-a-vis the epistemic phenomena and experiential realities surrounding and impinging on his sentient soul. In this sense, poetry is a passive receptacle to imbibe and register the vibrations received from *within* and *without*, from an orchestration of inner sensations and external stimuli. Its rhetorical beauty, cadence and melody spring naturally to the poems just as buds spring spontaneously to the flowering twigs. Therefore, poetry is more instinctual than any intellect-driven activity. Younas's poems, as assorted here so prudently by Sunita Grover Raina, nicely presents this romantic ideation of poetry as a divine and inspirational activity which is exclusively the *forte* of the poet *per se*.

At this point it is too tempting to resist quoting again from Younas's opening poem:

If the phase of young age had to part with me
If happy moments were meant to flee
If dark ends are showcased by destiny
So, what?
No, however, no but
For I am there to very much agree
With all that is nature's or God's decree

The lines as cited above betray the invincible journey of the soul towards eternity, setting aside nonchalantly the challenges to the body wrought by *Time* - the frowns of ageing, and the dark ends showcased by destiny. The poet's bold iteration, So, what? stems from an absolutely unconditional resignation to God's decree. Here poetry transcends the *physical* and encompasses a *messianic* vision, which is what Rishi Aurobindo Ghosh defines in his book, *The Future Poetry* in terms of *divine illumination* beyond being an assemblage of words and metaphors tempered with stylistic oeuvres. Considered stylistically, Younas writes with an unimpeded lyrical fluency, a limpid lyrical flow that comes easily to everyman's heart, and nestles there with a long lingering resonance. Younas's simplicity in versification is delightfully deceptive. Underlying the placid and transparent text is a hidden core of meaning that the French film critic Jean Mitry, on reading into it, would have presumably characterised as the type and symbol of *higher language*. I leave out mentioning the other poems of this book and leave them to the prospective readers to explore, to sense their beauty, and to experience the delight of discovering the deep structures of visions in the subtext, which is what Jean Mitry calls the aesthetics of *higher language*. In fine, what is poetry but the lexically rhythmic rendering of a subtle wink of thought or just a deeply-felt emotion or a heightened sensation that distils the soul, and funnels to the reader as simply an impression that lifts him or her from the existential angst as long as its effect does not peter out! In this Younas excels by far the run-of-the-mill range of poets we come across these days. I look forward to a truly rewarding success of this debut publication of Younas Rehman's English poetry presented to us by Sunita Grover Raina.

Jay Basu

Birth of this book

Never in my life had I thought that one day I would write poetry. However, it happened. Destiny drags you to do things; of which you had, had not even a glimpse in your dreams. Poetry! I never wanted to read, but poetry caught me in the year 2021. I do read now, but instead I became addicted to writing poetry.

I will be honest that till this day, I have not been able to appreciate the work of many poets. I would rather say that I do not understand them. However, it is not that I cannot be attracted to poetry. This became true when I started reading online many poets and one day came across a poet, who wrote from his heart. His every poem and every line touched me. I, in my heart said that this is what poetry truly is. This is the poetry I like.

Strange, so strange, that I started collecting his poems and became his ardent fan. His poems may be long or appear unending, but I could never halt for a break and never got tired. Gradually, it became my wish to preserve his poems so that they do not land up in a dustbin, as it is not the nature of this poet to take care of his work. He takes poetry casually and expresses his feelings; maybe it makes his heavy heart lighter. His poems reflect his craving, his pining for someone or a certain type of life he wished to live with someone, but it did not happen. To me, he appears an enlightened soul.

He has been writing in Pashto language since his young days and those poems too are sad. He started writing in English in 2018 and entered the hearts of many. I started writing poetry in 2021, and this is when I came across his poems in various online forums. Slowly I interacted with him and realised that he writes, posts his poems and forgets about it. This was the beginning of this book. I compiled and tried my best to edit some of his poems, which I gathered from online forums and his FB profile. Actually, all I did was align the lines of his poems, did some punctuation work and made the layout a bit appealing.

Since this is the first time I took up such a task of editing, let me share some of my views about it. Specifically, about the usage of punctuation in poems. I have observed many ways of punctuation being followed. Different poets have different explanations to state on this subject. Finally, two things that I kept in mind while editing were:

1) Whatever be the style, the meaning of the poem should be clear to the reader, and 2) Too much of punctuation made the poem look ugly.

I have seen at times that long sentences are broken into parts by some poets and every part starts with a capital letter; however, the feel of continuity does not exist. It seems prose has been snipped to convert to poetry. This leaves a bad taste in the mouth and the poem's layout looks ugly too. This peculiar snipping makes the poem difficult to understand. Well, these are my observations and views, and I might be totally wrong in my analyses.

Further I take pride in stating; I also designed the front and back cover of this book as I did not want anyone to have anything to do with this book. That shows the possessive and jealous nature of this fan.

Dr Jaysankar Basu is a highly respected poet who also loves Younas Rehman and whom I requested to do the foreword of this book, for I knew, I would not have been able to give due justice to Younas Rehman's poems. Loving his poems is one thing, but expressing its depth in a beautiful way is a skill I lack. So, I approached the master, my dear brother, Dr Jaysankar Basu. I had to accept this with a heavy heart, just joking. This also shows that this fan understands her limitations and wanted the best. My dada (brother) understands me well, loves me and is ever forgiving. Pranam dada.

Let me highlight some more of my drawbacks even though I am deviating from the main subject. Flowery, beautiful, impressive and touching language does not come to me as my vocabulary is limited, or rather my vocabulary became tuned to my career of 37 years. I don't like to struggle for words when it comes to doing work of prose or poetry. I write in the same way as I speak. My poems are therefore simple. I understand simple poetry only. This is also the reason I never considered myself apt to be a moderator, admin or group expert. I am, though, an expert in filing court petitions, affidavits, appeals and confusing people. Use of proper punctuations on such documents is an art I excel in; which can change the verdict. Applicable for poetry too; as improper punctuation or lack of punctuation can distort the meaning of the poem. However, for poetry, I feel it should be just enough to get the right meaning across.

In this birth, let me stick to writing poetry, if it can be termed poetry; maybe in next birth, I will be writing prose too. Though I have a feeling this is my last birth. Hope you all will understand my dilemma and pardon me for any mistakes you come across in this book. Love to all of you.

Sunita Grover Raina

-1-

I Write It, And Then I Erase It Myself

Eventually
I should draw a picture of mine
That refutes the prints of decline
Upon my visage
Woes did their best to rob me of rest
And now it is my turn to ward them away
Things are destined to flee, meant never to stay
If the phase of young age had to part with me
If happy moments were meant to flee
If dark ends are showcased by destiny
So, what?
No, however, no but
For I am there to very much agree
With all that is nature's or God's decree
And now I turn to vibes of love
O, love you played with mortals so far
You deceived the hearts that looked at stars
Even in broad daylight when the sun was shining
You played havoc with yearnings that kept on pining
For someone loved

But how long illusion can reign supreme?
How long would vanity maintain its theme?
Love too is mortal, and so is deceit
Nothing is perfect, nothing complete
Replete with rifts are notions and thoughts
I saw in life all colds and hots
And no more would I ever be bought
By the sweetness of images and glimmering mirages
I can live alone as I lived before
As a beggar, I can knock at any other door
If one door is closed
And my friends, I would say that come what may
Mention of breezes of spring can no longer stay
A means of solace or zone of delight
Let me then go with my relativist plight
Day and night will alternate as before
And all things, I shall forget as before
I would not knock at a glamorous door
My humble cottage, my plain lifestyle
I prefer to placements pompous and royal
I am neither a Prince nor a legendary figure
I am humble and frail with all things meagre
Since these are mine and borrowed from none
I love them as they have faithfully done
All they could do to keep me composed
With comparisons, I won't let things exposed
That bears witness to my having been frail
In whims and fancies, I would far better dwell
If they can bring me an unborrowed joy
I hadn't requested my God to create me
So why not alone, my friends you let me

To decide for myself whatever I do
With my tears and sweat drops, I will bring a new hue
To my orchards, my gardens, my sands of time
And I am free from, caring for rhymes
For I never claim to have been a poet
I say what I think to be exhausted from my heart
I never intend to ink a piece of art
If I have spoken at length, let it not
Be considered as an offshoot of thought
That I want to prolong what needs no dilation
I amuse myself and need no admiration
For what I say
For who can listen to a far-off yell
Devoid of beauty, charm and spell
I am a slogan; I raise it myself
I write it and then I erase it myself.

©Younas Rehman

-2-

Ever With Me

He regretted
But after an unduly big lapse of time
he did notice
After so much delay the unmatching rhyme
that was uttered somehow in my haphazard lines
So, it happens this way
That wounds bleed but get noticed after procrastination
And such was likewise the fate of my passions
In total obscurity I most often dwell
And at times I sink in my weird imagery
Coupled with thinking that realities shall
always remain obscure and arcane
Much distant from vision and beyond the domain
of my poor cognition
Some ideas however
That might envision me to open the closures
That so far could not get a chance for exposure
Did come to my mind
Yet
I had to forget what I thought I can't get
For liberty means nothing in face of hard fate

And so being the state of affairs, I face
And the picture of things that come in my sight
I can hardly decide as to what went wrong
And what substitution might have been right

Ok
That isn't a matter that has some significance
Let me now build up a new domain
Of thought that allows me to do what I can
I know
That never in my life could I ever know
As to how many I's have assembled together
To make an impression of my being a one "I"
Trillions of cells, each with its own full existence
Shrink into unity, diversity and distance
They are born, they assemble, multiply and die
And these glued together, make for me what am I
They tell me that how I am different from you
They tell me what is what and who is who
Let this mysterious discussion be over
Like a cloud let me wander and hover
Above my very self and my humble identity
If I am at all an existing reality
And the world can acknowledge my relativist propensity
For I am somewhat different from rest of humanity
With peculiar world view of happenings around
I have my own scales for judging affairs
As to which are amenable, rational and sound
And I
Apply
These parameters to desires as well

I have my own picture of heaven and hell
And now let me talk, my sweet comrade to you
Let's while away the remaining lot of time
In something interesting, some passion sublime
And that passion is nothing else than a craving
For having
You
Ever with me

©Younas Rehman

-3-

My Insane Dream

My insane dream has provoked my desire
Tantalising me with things that I can't acquire
Draining out all my perspicacity to see
As to what can't be I, and what I can be
O my insane illusion, how you will understand
That there is a reason that I nowhere stand
And that person hadn't been mine even before
Whose estrangement so painfully now you deplore
And as for assessment, we shall carry it later
That which are the causes that constantly scatter
My well weaved fabric of sweet aspirations
The flowers of yearnings, the orchards of passions
Dig not my present, as left nothing is there
About which to speak or about which to hear
So being the sad annals, let me speak to you too
O beloved of mine, O my old soul mate who
Has been steeped so deep in my memories sweet
With images of past that I cannot delete
My friends often tell me that people who leave
Won't turn back ever once they offer adieu
Despite these realities, I still take respite

In hoping that someday in future they might
Make up their mind to mingle again
With a saddened companion who to this day remains
Hopeful amidst all the hopeless dark mist
For seeing once again me, isn't that odd at least
And whether you come round or leave me for good
In each case so proud I feel that I could
Enjoy some time of having been together
With your good self in the bygone weather
Of spring days galore and flowers all around

©Younas Rehman

-4-

O Year Twenty, Twenty-Two!

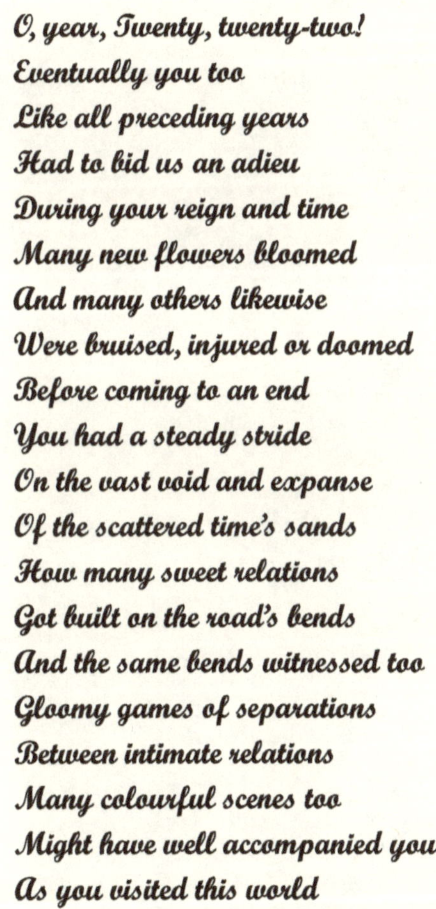

O, year, Twenty, twenty-two!
Eventually you too
Like all preceding years
Had to bid us an adieu
During your reign and time
Many new flowers bloomed
And many others likewise
Were bruised, injured or doomed
Before coming to an end
You had a steady stride
On the vast void and expanse
Of the scattered time's sands
How many sweet relations
Got built on the road's bends
And the same bends witnessed too
Gloomy games of separations
Between intimate relations
Many colourful scenes too
Might have well accompanied you
As you visited this world

And much passionate dreams also
Might have been hurled
And flung, shattered into pieces
Like smashed and broken glass
And when now a new year
Has dawned and glowed around
Let's pray that everywhere
Peace, tranquillity and love
Rule supreme and make a theme
Of otherwise banal life
That remains laden with strife
And barren, fruitless struggles
Let's hope, rather believe
That each day of the year new
Will play its role in heightening
Our courage and morale
Let's kneel, pray and call
Our Lord, the Lord of all
That this life brief and small
Be no more just a bin
Of garbage of dead time
Let's have our spirits
Elevated and sublime
Let's build over the ashes
Of cremated bygone time
A pretty new clime

Of a sweet and calm existence
That surmounts each resistance
Of odds and their hardship
Let's all believe strongly
In compassionate God's lordship.

©Younas Rehman

-5-

I Remember The Moments

I remember the moments when I meet someone else
Though words get forgotten, the accents still dwell
And whenever looked at by someone, by chance
I remember their face from the meaning of their glance
I shun and am shy of the social traditions
As I recall the shoulders on which I might be deemed
To have been an unwelcome, unwanted burden
As for bitter words uttered by someone to me
I delete them from mind with a remorseless glee
Yet from my mind, I can never delete
The bitter attitude with which others me treat.

©Younas Rehman

-6-

I Feel

I feel as though it is only you that I
Consider as life's each how and why
Though you had been never an acquaintance of mine
As stranger you came and became so much nigh
I feel as though all other wishes gave way
To a single most sway of a remotest ray
That sprouted somewhere in my destiny's sky
And then turned into twilight; on horizon of yearning
An edge where fire of desire is burning
It is now only you that I seek and pursue
As the final embodiment of fragrance and hue
It is not all you, as the world is much large
People come in and go with all glamour and fame
But see nonetheless so much deeply absorbed
In fathomless memories of yours I am
How specificity governs the world of our hearts
Just one beauty rules out all other arts
Of nature that abound in beauties galore
Then save that one being we chase nothing more
As for placement and stature that I can enjoy
In this coloured society, is never so high

As may catch the attention of somebody else
The tale of my being is what my countenance tells
As for you, you are deemed by many to be
Their fountain of joy, their source of glee
Let me tell you, my sweetheart! That my lot is humility
And yours is glamour, for ever, far ever
My love! I won't beg you to me a favour
For we are so different and much poles apart
You enjoy each right to forsake me and part.

-7-

My Own Feelings!

My own feelings!
I kept you suppressed and hidden from others
For who bothers
About what others feel
Yet for too long
I could not keep you hidden
For eyes know not
As to what is legitimate and what is forbidden
My eyes glowed with each of my woes
And as for now, each looker knows
The tumults that arise in the hidden corners
Of a pining heart that withers and bows
Down like a detached, cut off branch
I didn't tell them as to whom I love
Yet from the lines that at times I pen
Friends guess out all the secrets that remain
Hidden and obscure in my own presumption
Why not then I embrace a resumption
Of love and its vibes just open to all
For love can't be hidden behind a wall

Either of heart or some masquerading else
Love succumbs not to veiling, it itself tells
That it dost exist
So, I would no more resist
Its spontaneous flow
Its bursting into glow.

-8-

You Somehow Eventually Decided To

You somehow eventually decided to
Say bye to me with a heavy heart
Or perhaps even with no regret too
But can I ask as to whether I shall
Dwell on counting endless instants
Of living to myself away from you
Seasons will come and will get replaced
By still newer seasons of flavours and hue
With fresher songs of newly born
And grown-up songbirds coming in throngs
And when I hear them, so deeply I long
For revival of bygone moments when we
Would join to hear, listen and see
The colours around on plains and mounds
And under the lush, green, fragrant tree
Yea! Those were times of our life's prime

When each thing around would look sublime
And as for now, those colours decayed
And banality it is that endured and stayed.

-9-

All Is Best With Your Being As It Is

Being an average or an ordinary
Is not a bad word to describe you
Accept "As is" as it is too
Equivalent just to being par excellence
No
A potential and drive you have
All is best that your maker gave
You as part of your inner traits
Turn equal at last all sizes and weights
Torment not your ego and your self-imaging
By what others think, as you think, of you
Or what you wish to be your look and hue
All is best with your being as it is
Fantastic and good is everything as it is.

©Younas Rehman

-10-

O, Sacred Heart's Deep-Rooted Love!

O, sacred heart's deep-rooted love !
Before you I kneel, I humbly bow
By God, I have drunk many a time
Either alone or in sweetest company
Of my closest, most intimate friends
In clear climate and in cloudy weather
But I have never, by God, found that elation
That infatuating, soothing intoxication
As you gave me, just with your single glance
O my deep love for someone, some strange person
Whom I had never ever seen before
You are the leader, of each
enthralling drunkenness
At times I start calculating
hours and days
Months and years along my existence and ways
That I came across along with woe and glee
Which, hithertofore, I had not happened to see
When my erstwhile transparent heart was free
I count them, distil them and crystallize them

And assemble them into a tangible memory
Of love free bygone months and years
And then turn back to my present time
I calculate seconds and minutes too
In which my songs were addressed to you
O, God of both of us, me and my love
You stay witness at least to the very yeast
Of which a lover's heart had been made
And you observe that clot of clay as well
In which you instilled a love's fragrant smell
And produced therefrom an enchanting spell
That turns mad
The heart you'd made
I had to get burnt sometime, somewhere
Here or there, either far or near
It is ok that the flames that are burning me
Are blended and kneaded in attachment's wine
And when I drink it, the world becomes mine
I find an augmented, redoubled elation
O, sacred whisky! You enhance my passion
I swear by your intoxication
Your blessed and holy inebriation
That all this elation takes its hue
Only and only, just from you.

©Younas Rehman

-11-

With All This, I Had To Survive As Well

I had to seek you wherever I could
To this day from the early days of manhood
I had to pen down my life's tale
With all this, I had to survive as well

I had to bear with the pangs of difference
I own legitimacy of your indifference
But love will not care for heaven or hell
With all this, I had to survive as well

I could read a wild script in glow of your eyes
I knew how unreciprocated love dies
I saw that in dew drops and tears love dwells
With all this, I had to survive as well

I loved all the ambiance surrounding you
And feared as well as to what people do
When in love a solitary soul ever fell
With all this, I had to survive as well

Wisdom or vanity or just an illusion
The darkness of saddening, chill solitude
Or just a futility of my attitude
Something had cast an inebriating spell
With all this, I had to survive as well

I knew the secret of ceaseless alternation
Of seasons, days and nights in succession
Union would also witness segregation
Parting finally tolls a failing love's knell
With all this, I had to survive as well.

©Younas Rehman

-12-

I Will Love All The Same

At times in this city, at others in another city
I sought you, using each shred of my perspicacity
At nights thoughts about you haunted my sleep
And on days, I treaded either this or that street
Either love or the beauty, one of them was so deep
Neither I could advance, not could ever I retreat
At times I thought all I thought was an illusion
And better than a company could've been seclusion
But now things are different and I see an equivalence
Being or being not with you, each thing is delusion
Amidst these circumstances, on a standstill I live
With threads of my feelings some dreamlands I weave
But feelings are feelings and dreams remain dreams
Never meant to be true are my yearnings and themes
I am alien to this land, an unfamiliar stranger
This land is not mine, it belongs to me not
With a tinge of being unheard as a far-off frail cry
I am just nothing more than an offshoot of thought
Fraught with some pains are my hidden regrets
Impervious to love songs and anthems of hate

I was bound to weep as and when I recalled you
And I lost you whenever my ballads enthralled you
Each time with sad songs of mine I called you
How can I own you when so different we are
I am like a bubble while you are a star
With all these my dear, I will keep on recalling
The green springy leaves which are now down falling
If present can't own me, I will live in past
Irrespective of what was retained, what was lost
For love is embraced as a lifelong game
You may alienate me; I will love all the same.

-13-

I Am A Woman

I am a woman
Just as your own mother
Whom you revere as your sacred mom
But I being not your mom, am just a woman
Though I am married, a sacred trust for my hubby
Yet for common man
I am looked upon as a play thing for hobby
I am out on road heading towards a market
To buy some bread as many males do
I am not adorned with some special hue
I am dressed in ordinary clothes too
With no provocative cuts or carves
But see
It is the seventh car that passes by me
That chases me, halts and asks me
Whether I am alone
With motives bad he further adds,
"Come on and just sit inside
I will treat you like my bride
Let's have an excursion outside

and enjoy a luxurious time
I will buy you things of your choice "
I see the fumes of lust in his voice
I turn aside my humble eyes
And reach a bread shop just nearby
Now it is early hours of the night
Lamps are lit bright and all things are in sight
That baking man is now gazing at me
Adding further to my apprehension and fright
He is looking at me with suggestive gesture
Taking fullest survey of my curves and vesture
As he hands me the bread, he touches my hands
As if I've been his own girlfriend
I ignore all these things and humbly pass on
Then another car comes up, and halts on my way
Its driver asks me as to how much he should pay
For my staying with him for a night or a day
This is my land
That was carved on name of a religious yell
But instead of paradise, it is sending to hell
Its weaker inhabitants
I am silent and quiet, for I lack manly might
I am unable to speak, I am helpless and weak
To my garments, gets stuck up a tiny taint too
But a man would lose nothing if his grave sins leak
Shame is for women and pride for men
If to sex and sexuality matters pertain

Here women are treated as second rate slaves
Here each man is libertine, who proudly craves
For sex irrespective of honour or shame
But such things are horrible and never forgiven
If labelled get these on poor woman's name.

©Younas Rehman

-14-

My Love, I Wish You Aren't Annoyed

Though many a plaint may create a tide
On the seashore of your beautiful heart
You may opt to weep and make me weep
You may plunge and burry my ego deep
In marshes of regrets and painful remorse
Whatever feelings you may show or hide
My love I wish you are not annoyed
At times I might forget you too
And without you too, the fragrance and hue
Of ambiance around might keep me sound
Then steer my memory and make me recall
The bygone moments when the events all
Circled around our love and pride
My love I wish you are not annoyed
Bring to your mind that romantic weather
That bonded two separate souls together
To a single passion we remained allied
My love I wish you are not annoyed
At times words may not be able to
Express the vibes that I have for you

In that case, try to become my voice
When we think alike, each thing is nice
A feeling of oneness is our only guide
My love I wish you are not annoyed.

©Younas Rehman

-15-

Neither A Ray Of Light Could I Be

Neither a ray of light could be I
To sooth the yearnings of someone's eye
Nor could any mortal's heart be ever
Cooled with listless song of mine
A lump of clay sans colour, sans fragrance
A being that wins no warm remembrance
Myself in pain, how could I ever gain
A name for alleviating someone else's pain
Beauties sprouted galore in each colour and tinge
But on the disk of destiny, I remained on its fringe
And nobody could ever condescend to look
At me with bewitching, spell binding looks
A fallen leaf floating I am on the brooks
That flow in some distant and unnoticed lands
I remained an alien, unnoticed, unknown
Even to the very self that I own
On some far-off cliff like a thorny bush
Away from limelight was I stealthily grown
I live somewhere, neither here nor there

Agony, anguish, uncertainty and fear
Are things I face and see everywhere
The One thing I shared with all fellow men
Was time that passed independent and same
On all the lucky ones and on all the wretched
On anonymous chaps and on fortunate ones
Who printed on sands of time their name
But that time as well with me couldn't dwell
It too had eventually to bid me farewell
And when time pops up in a spring laden weather
The autumn struck leaves I pick up and gather
I am like a tomb of my dead aspirations
And scattered ashes of my cremated passions.

Younas Rehman

-16-

At Last, I Had To

At last, I had to leave for some quiet
Place of retreat, so that I might
Heave sigh of relief, after many a toil
With a recompensed glow of a contented smile
I wish for a while I may visit a loyal
Some solitary place of serene solitude
And find for myself a composed attitude
After voyaging long on the sands of age's time
As bygone stays those sweet days of my prime
I require a rest, a seclusion at its best
Assuming eventually, I've cleared the test
That life had given me in its early tenure
I endured bravely what I could endure
And now totally broken, fallen and shaken
I think I have to be silently taken
To a place of rest with no zeal and zest
A stage where loneliness and silence are best.

-17-

Oh, That Dreams Could Lose Their Grip

Oh, that dreams could lose their grip
On all of my passions living deep
In the deep recesses of my care worn heart
How many of these dreams have already robbed
My heart of peace and hopes that throbbed
Like springy breezes and fervour's glow
Oh, these dreams have become so much agonising
The dreams that so far I had been patronising
And eventually all of them got proved to be
Nothing more but a mirage and agony
Many a yearnings were source of burning
For my tender heart that relied on earning
Happiness in things that I so much desired
But happiness from nowhere else can be hired
Then from things that we already have with us
Joy can't be borrowed from things that lie
Out of reach and accessible not
Fling each thought than regrettably rot
In whimsical wishes and unfulfilled desires
Yet all these dreams are not at least

Devoid totally of fervour and flair
At times they take us to bending road
Where destinies kiss the success of affair
My love it is true that I couldn't get you
My dreams have nonetheless given me a clue
To have some ephemeral, pleasant escape
From distress, bonding me in agony's trap.

©Younas Rehman

-18-

Now A Stage Has Begun

When two distinctly separate entities
Blend somehow into a single unity
Such as your heart is there with you
But from your beloved it borrows its hue
Then a pretty spectacle is there being seen
That a merger of two beings your soul has been
When yours are the ears but these eagerly hear
The words that she utters here or there
And whenever you breathe, you feel the fragrance
Deep in your soul, of her springy presence
Then amidst all the beauties surrounding you
All that you sense, think of and do
Is a search of attaining a strange destination
In journey of craving, yearning and passion
Then it is a phase in which your every gaze
On a fixed single point grazes and stays
And one overwhelming being there remains
In your heartbeats, mind and veins
As a sovereign power
That just overpowers
All other things

At times when utterly you are occupied
And all of a sudden, some image that you hide
Triggers your mind to remember someone
In dictionary of love your job has been done
When your sleepless night is just over
And a twilight of reddening lines cover
Your sleepy eyes
Amidst unheard sighs
Then know you are caught up in an endless connection
It is time to end up each procrastination
And warmly blend up each feeling and passion
This once been done, now a stage has begun
That be your own, get scared of none
And the one you love should be openly told
That her in your heart you ceaselessly hold.

©Younas Rehman

-19-

It Still Infatuates My Soul And Heart

It still infatuates my soul and heart
Whenever I hear the magic of sound
That springs and echoes in world around
And the sound made by your tender steps
While walking along that narrow track
On the bank of a beauteous, deep, blue lake
Where sometime we had for the first time met

It still infatuates my soul and heart
Whenever a smile glows on your face
I still remember each mark and trace
That earliest talks of ours had made
On the echoing ambiance and nearby trees
I still remember that enlivening breeze
That made your long hair toss in air
The words you said by then are still

Filled with thrill of a pleasant feel
All these were but destined to go
Away with the tides of the time's flow

It still infatuates my soul and heart
Whenever I recall the colour and fragrance
Of the first-ever meeting that left its remembrance
In my heart for ever as a source of joy
A feel that needs no how and why

It still infatuates my soul and heart
Whenever I see you in a pleasant mood
Or even annoyed, impudent and rude
In each act of yours, I see a charm
Be it a kindness or an act of harm
I love each thing you say or do
The simple reason is I still love you

It still infatuates my soul and heart
Whenever I write on my palm your name
Even since long is over the game
Of the bygone stages of love and romance
For nature may not repeat its chance
That youth had granted us sometime once
Each hope and chance is for ever lost
To go back into the irretrievable past

But whatever the vicissitudes of time be
I adamantly stand to sense a glee
In all things that somehow relate to thee

It still infatuates my soul and heart
It still infatuates my soul and heart.

-20-

The Grand Scheme Of Life

The grand scheme of life would not gain any good
From the malice we harbour and the grudges we brood
Given that we are just mortals, not saints
With peculiar traits and weak mental bents
Nobody is perfect, free from making mistakes
Inside frailty we all have our stakes
At some points of time, we afflict many others
Our nearest ones and our co human brothers
We are not saints, we should gracefully own
That we commit mistakes, both known and unknown
We need not blame others, who must be forgiven
For errors these are to which mortals are driven
Each road and each pathway of life is bending
That call for good vibes and a good understanding
Of what humans are, how they succumb to ills
No one's life is garden of comforts and thrills
The act of forgiveness isn't only an act
Of kindness to others, rather it has impact
On rebuilding ourselves into quite new versions
Of our very selves that face an immersion
Into depths of stiff wildness that stiffens life's course

Let's save ourselves from subsequent remorse
When we remake ourselves by grudges got released
Love is brought round and annoyance appeased
Our souls we unshackle from the load of resentment
Human climate gets softened and sensations get pleased
We should not think of ourselves as victims even if
Seasons look as autumnal and pale gets every leaf
Not cycle of blame should ever we perpetuate
Ill times may be taken as some lessons of fate
Knowledge means to acknowledge the value of norms
We are far supreme humans, not a crowd of worms
Through an active will for our prosperous growth
We should remake ourselves into our best versions
Fostering healthy relations and a sweet positivity
Or else life will succumb to doom of calamity.

©Younas Rehman

-21-

My Heart Keeps Burning

My friends, advise me not
To extinguish the fire
That keeps aglow my bruised heart
Nor tell me the art
Of assembling the pieces
Of my sundered heart
For I can't search for
And collect its pieces
One by one
You won't comprehend
What the heart does stand
For
The heart that assembles
All its ambiance
The heart that gathers
The Sun, the moon and the stars
All these luminous entities burn
To earn
Some light, some fire and some glow
My friends, you won't know
That hearts too burn like them

To get a flame
Inside its deep recesses
To break and shatter into pieces
Just to earn some lovely kisses
From poetic lines
Thus, the game of flame is ancient indeed
And each one segment
Of my broken heart
Is a blazing Sun in its own being
That illuminates everything
Around it
My heart! My pride, my own Sun
I have begun
Adoring you
I will keep you burning, ablaze for ever
To fade out never
To die out never.

-22-

Neither You Could Speak Out, Nor I Could Say

I had so much longed for your company, yet
It is alright if it could not be met
Even I faced it the way it went
And you too got what you had meant
I spent my life as whatever it was and you likewise your life spent
I see times and seasons are insipid now
And no more has that intimacy remained
The winds move slowly and moonlit nights
Have lost their charm, colours and sprites
And our relation is a dead cessation
With no more earlier warmth of passion
Neither I could speak, nor could you ever leak
The reason behind the procrastination
That finally brought an end to relation
That had once bloomed with sweet aspiration
Went on these events of baffling deadlocks
Neither moved you were, nor moved was I
And none of us ever raised the question
That all these could occur eventually why
This way both of us indifferent remained

And no commonality could get entertained
You urged, that forward I should move
And mine was ego, that it should be you
To revive our old intimacy again
Neither you could speak out, nor I could say
That where eventually we're destined to stay.

-23-

Just Silently All These I Hear And See

Just silently all these I hear and see
Whatever come and whatever these be
I hear your name with all of its glam
Being mentioned before me whatever I am
With pain my heart sighs with all unheard cries
And these float on the ocean of tears that dries
When eyes are tired of looking around
In futile hopes from the hard, barren ground
Of false expectations and unheard supplications
These are fruits of my fruitless sensations
Oh, that I could be just impervious to things
That bring nothing else than despair that clings
To the chambers of my heart that glow hot like ambers
Yet I can find a good reason then too
That dark shadows as well can eventually prove
As heralders of some far-off reminiscent light
That over at last will be this scary night
For vicissitudes of times and fate

Won't give eternity to woes that frustrate
Nights pass on, days come and sun shines again
Nothing in this world forever remain.

-24-

Just Have Faith

Nothing is odd, nothing is strange
The urge for happiness is genuine and candid
The only issue relating thereto
Lies in mislocation of things
Certain things are located here
While many others lie else somewhere
And as for happiness that perishes not
Must be looked for, chased and sought
In location other than the planet earth
Where you have got your organic birth
But pleasures and happiness lie ahead
In the world to come that you sillily dread
Or even doubt its very existence
For your vision can't surmount the resistance
Offered by your protoplasmic mesh
That encages you and holds you in
Obscuring from you the grander space
That stands transcendental to all you amass
For gratifying your urge for happiness
Which however does not exist there
Where you think it might be found

Raise your head above the ground
And see that earth isn't the only place
Heaven is far more superior in grace
God didn't make you one of the species
To die, decay and perish for good
You deserve far more, just have faith
And after last you take your breath
You would be given a life that doesn't end
On vast expanse of time's sand.

©Younas Rehman

-25-

O My Heart!

O my heart!
Have you too parted with me
Did you not bear to see me in glee
Were my dreams nothing but a purposeless vanity
Or wilfully you took them just for insanity
My heart! It isn't you to decide what is good
My vanity, as you deem it, may be baseless and crude
But I tell you these dreams were amazingly sweet
These turned my existence with joys replete
I won't part with them even though these are false
For without them chances of survival look scarce
I am like that beggar that sits under a tree,
Collects fallen dry leaves ensure and see
That these are from danger of being scattered free
Now you too my sweetheart may listen from me
It isn't a matter of affliction or glee
I love you because the same love is my cause
I will remain a lover, as I previously was

My bygone past and my forthcoming future
Are destined to remain dedicated to thee
I will buy each agony with a sweet surprise
If only I could sell my pleasures and joys.

-26-

For Love Isn't A Fruit Of Season

Love, if true, won't wait for rhymes
Written and sung on certain times
For love isn't a fruit of season
All climes are but attachment's climes
Convergence of times on a single instant
Is a rule on which love plays its game
Shrinking of space into a single point
Is yet the passion's second name
Be it December or the chill month of January
Be it a specified day of February
Love won't attach its mark to certain
Days or places under focused reverie
As places are just a continuum only
Of one earth that we know as world
So are blended even times all
To make a continuous life's journey
The dust of lust of rusting hearts
Fly and settle on pathways chosen
But heart to heart bonds have their own horizons

Beyond the limits that lust demands
Love cries eternally with a single yell
That let's remain each other's beau and belle
Much far beyond the day of valentine
And say I'm yours and you're mine.

-27-

Where Passions Get Unrestricted Flights

Below the cables
Where clouds soar and roar with praise of God
I weave my thoughts within poetic knots
For inside the arcane words and tones
Open up dances with fervour and alacrity
O, the annal of my life!
You are an unmatched tale of strife
I use my ink and pen and a silent voice
I chase the echo resonating in heavens
So distant and so distant though
My soul takes pride in the words that I weave
Into songs of mine that capture vast moments
Through moments that I dedicate to them
For poetry is the asset that can rightly claim
It being belonging to the echoing hearts
Where passions get unrestricted flights
Free from fears and restraining frights
In each of my couplets, some part of mine
Is part of the words that burst into chime
I write these all for the world around

So, it is free, not slavishly bound
To restricting forces or halting thought
For less than freedom is anything not
Suiting my lot.

-28-

Undefined Love

So often I coerce my mind to think otherwise
And repeat with myself that my love won't rise
To an uncommon and surprising level
Yet whenever you are not with me,
I feel that old wounds may eventually be
On the way to getting healed at last
I struggle to think that I am free
From the clutches of unmet, craving love
For someone who may not be having love
To the same degree in return for me
I reiterate that I shall forget
The place and time where we had met
And start assuming that I am free
Like a forlorn far off lonely tree,
From winds and breezes of social life
If only it proves not a fruitless strife
But how to believe it!
A thought that haunts me, a pledge that daunts me
An idea that perhaps she also wants me
Neither I can wipe it, nor someway retrieve it
A strange hallucination, what name to give it

Perhaps this half-dead love will at last
Gather some strength and burst with a blast
I try to speak as much less as possible
But what to do with the echoing song
That resonates in my vibes for a long
Yea those are the words that I had heard
From your sweet self some time ago
And like streamlets still, they flow
From the same venue where we had met
I try to sleep in slumber so deep
That no past thought would be able to creep
Into my memory and recollections
But nature's anthems are perpetually sung
And somehow to this day, I remain clung
To thoughts and imageries all about you
Let me revisit this maize of attachment
Let me renovate this phase of attachment
For if forgetting can never be true
Then I should carry on remembering you.

©Younas Rehman

-29-

My Love After All We Are Two Different Souls

I could never turn the times in my favour
Futile was each effort, vain stood each endeavour
Now I think of customising and taming my mind
To meshes and loops that cannot unwind
Let me congratulate them who beat me in battle
I would boldly applaud them who defeat me in battles
Apart from what goes on between myself and others
Let me talk to you also, dear sweetheart at last
I'm neither a volcanic being that would blast,
Nor a luminous star
That would shine for ever
I lay already buried beneath the chill frost
Of being unattended, an uncalled-for existence
And now no more I care for odds and resistance
If still you acknowledge my attachment for you
Then still likewise you will find me too
Waiting for you and adorning for you
Each evening for you and each morning for you
And when it is so that you need me no more
No later than thought of, you may close every door

That leaves some access to what went on before
One thing at least let me humbly submit
A one-time plight that I will not repeat
That I may be heard with a cool mind once
Before we say bye to each thought of romance
And dismantle the long-cherished mystery of love
For some credit is owed to long history of love
I promise I won't go beyond due limits
I know what are norms and revered constraints
You may give up loyalty rejecting my fealty
I harbour at heart no regrets or complaints
I know how to handle and tame my emotions
I know how to deal with my inward commotions
And you also know how to chase your goals
My love after all we are two different souls.

-30-

Love It Is

Love is one of the noblest passions
Resting its existence on plain of sensation
It substantiates itself in each living being
If it has its consciousness and an ego's tinge
Love isn't a feeling, yet it creates
Many a feeling and passions galore
Love like a student reads its own history
And tries to search out and explore
As to how it began, where and when
And how to maintain it each now and then
It isn't a sensation, yet of sure it is
An originator of a mix of passions
Love is a consequence of events in sequence
First some amusement a soul aspires for
Some beauty to see, sometime of glee
Some solacing plea for amusing one's soul
And then a liking for someone develops
Where seeing and talking pleasantly envelopes
The so far free soaring carefree thought
But this liking stops here not
It keeps on going through next transitions

Here the liking gets ranked as ambitions
A strong ambition to have someone
For mirth and fervour as a charming fun
Thus, liking changes into a strong desire
Which is yet unconscious of getting on fire
When desire ripens, it becomes an attachment
One feels one's soul is without thrill
Until some beautiful company is had
Here it is, the desire gets red
With heat of its constantly growing intensity
It is the phase that desire now has
Changed into yearning with passions hot burning
Now having a chance to cast just a glance
Looks overpowering like starting romance
This is a linkage, a tuning of soul
For subsuming one's self and life's course whole
Into a strong, irresistible longing
Longing when reaches its ultimate goal
Here it is that one finds one's soul
Fully submerged into depth of belonging
That is the ultimate destiny of longing
Which so at one step we term as love
Love may then undergo many turns
At times it cools, at other it burns
Love starts alternating as days and nights do
Love starts appearing in each possible hue
Love is linked invariantly with sentiments too
And yet in itself, it is not an emotion
It retains its domain with all exclusivity
It shapes up and reshapes its non-stop activity
It can make allowance for due perversity

It can opt for assuming any shape of diversity
Love is in all forms most prized passion
Though it can't be defined in specific narration
Like an artist, it prints its own paintings
Not only in souls, minds and hearts
But also, on the vast nature's pieces of art
Be it a visage of some beautiful person
Or the cool beaming rays of a calm moonlit night
Whatever be the annals of season
Whatever be the slogan of reason
Love would remain adamantly clung
To songs that norms may not have sung
Love often infuses its flavour and sprite
In each thing related to vibes of love
Love is a lively, living reality
It breathes, grows, speaks and responds
Love tends to lodge its peculiar demands
First of which is its being recognised
Its greatest ambition is its own recognition
Love has its own mathematics and ethics
Addition, subtraction, edition and deletion
Each thing love takes up with its peculiar break ups
Using its principles of norms and discretion.

©Younas Rehman

-31-

He Regretted

He regretted
But after an unduly big lapse of time
He did notice
After so much delay the unmatching rhyme
That was uttered somehow in my haphazard lines
So, it happens this way
That wounds bleed but get noticed after procrastination
And such was likewise the fate of my passions
In total obscurity I most often dwell
And at times I sink in my weird imagery
Coupled with thinking that realities shall
Always remain obscure and arcane
Much distant from vision and beyond the domain
Of my poor cognition
Some ideas however
That might envision me to open the closures
That so far could not get a chance for exposure
Did come to my mind
Yet
I had to forget what I thought I can't get
For liberty means nothing in face of hard fate

And so being the state of affairs I face
And the picture of things that come in my sight
I can hardly decide as to what went wrong
And what substitution might have been right
Ok
That's isn't a matter that has some significance
Let me now build up a new domain
Of thought that allows me to do what I can
I know
That never in my life could I ever know
As to how many I's have assembled together
To make an impression of my being a one " I "
Trillions of cells, each with its own full existence
Shrink into unity diversity and distance
They are born, they assemble, multiply and die
And these glued together make for me what am I
They tell me that how I am different from you
They tell me what is what and who is who
Let this mysterious discussion be over
Like a cloud let me wander and hover
Above my very self and my humble identity
If I am at all an existing reality
And the world can acknowledge my relativist propensity
For I am somewhat different from the rest of humanity
With peculiar worldview of happenings around
I have my own scales for judging affairs
As to which are amenable, rational and sound
And I
Apply
These parameters to desires as well
I have my own picture of heaven and hell

And now let me talk, my sweet comrade to you
Let's while away the remaining lot of time
In something interesting, some passion sublime
And that passion is nothing else than a craving
For having
You
Ever with me.

©Younas Rehman

-32-

We Are All Probabilities

Admitted that I have been crestfallen though
You too feel the sadness with which the winds blow
I am broken indeed but you too likewise
Aren't you the same as you were long ago
I may look like a piece of a broken ship's wreckage
Your eyes too then shine with a teary glow
Sad alone I am not in this city deserted
In each direction do the same feelings flow
And the scorching heat that agonises my soul
Is shared likewise by many around
Your future is also not far from being dark
If you find no spark in my humble background
I own
I don't own the sweet fragrance of breezes
With eternal spring's fragrance, you too aren't crowned
If I am a shadow of some unseen assumption
You too aren't free from the fortuitous function
Of the time that flows and bows never before
Even those whom we so persistently adore
If I am a chance, just a vain shred of thought
Then you too, my beloved, couldn't fill your lot

With beauty eternal and unwithering charm
We are all probabilities that loom everywhere
Conjectures prevail, no certainty stays here
Let pride be thrown off, for life is brief
Destined to wither is each flower and leaf
My love, let us value the joys of time
Let's share our feelings in each season and clime
I plight my allegiance and wish it is acknowledged
Before I am done with the end of my time.

-33-

If Only It Had Been Ever Possible For Me

If only it had been ever possible for me
I would have plucked off the radiance of stars
And fixed them on walls of the desolate nights
But I can't govern the events and sights
Of which I'm myself a tiny small part
Apart from what I entertain in my heart
My love, we defeated each other in vain
Better instead, if the aimless fight had
Been fought not between us, but with others around
In that case defeat too would have been sound
I charge you never for some mistake whatever
Nor for anything else that went anyway wrong
Neither you were disloyal nor could I ever long
For any disruption or disturbance to ties
That were built in the dreamland of teary eyes
We both lost this battle, but it isn't that fatal
For winning at times may prove worse than defeat
At least we can hope for a happy retreat
Neither you, nor can I ever know the distinction
Between the realities and the much-cherished fiction

Of fibres of time that bring up tomorrows
In lap of sweet pleasures or thorns of sorrows
Time dissociates us and assembles us too
Life differs from us but resembles us too

Can one thing with meaning be shared with you
I say if you stay for a few days more
Some plausible reason we may both explore
As to what is in front and behind the door
Of the chamber of destiny that has ever been
An unseen love's future, an unnoticed scene.

-34-

As We Sit On Stairs Of Life And Talk

With all its charms, allurements and joys
Spreading from earth's crust to heights of skies
And all its beauties that soothe yearning eyes
Love has one dark and saddening guise too
As we sit on stairs of life and talk
As we leisurely on some acquainted lanes walk
We notice how swiftly moments gather into hours
And get dumped so unnoticedly into bygone past
And many such moments to attachment get lost
Nor moments, but whole lot of this temporary sojourn
May phrase up to mean that we have to burn
Either in this love or that love somewhere
And feelings so irrevocably urge to adhere
To beauties around, to unflinching attractions
So passes this life in the grip of distractions
O, love for some person, you may take just one moment
Or many years together to build your stature
And once you start blooming, you groom our nature
Into wholesome belonging and unlimited longing
Then comes up the stage that each feature of life

Gets printed on its countenance your signature
When love solemnly embarks on land of existence
Then things reshape themselves for new things to learn
To unlearn others, and for new things to yearn
We lend new vistas to meaning of passions
We borrow new ideas from scope of relations
Some lovers grow flowers in flowerpots and vases
Some others get stuck and entangled in mazes
Some get their love fulfilled in smiles and joys
And some pass through melancholic and teary phases
Some insanes resort to comfort their yearnings
Through writing some poems that are read perhaps never
While some lovers find their likes somewhere
To share with them the cold flow of sad tears
My Lord, I know well, you deserve all love
For each beauty, each glamour is your creation
But I can't get to you as you aren't accessible
I can love your artwork that at least remains traceable
So, through these stunning beauties I should search for some pathway
That gets me to know your glory and honour
May be a few good looks of a sweetheart
Make me realise to open my eyes
To look at the distant domains above skies
And find the One Who created such glamours
From where arise the affairs de amour.

©Younas Rehman

-35-

I Am A Solitary Song

My sweet friend, how could you ever know
The agonies of nights kept vigil in remembrance
On one side eyes remain filled with tears
On other side silence where no one hears
But I complain not of what passes on me
Even in sad nights I see fragments of glee
Though I can't get you, how can I forget you
For even false dreams are an asset of joy
Which with venom of realism I can't destroy
You aren't with me, nor so you could be
For I am that unfortunate creature of God
Who if wishes a rainfall, will meet sparks of fire
I know how fate plays with and slays my desires
But I won't retreat, I will keep on my journey
On lands of attachment and would urge for a company
Even if no one would ever stand by me
I tell you, my sweetheart, love too is an art
It keeps the heart's orchards evergreen in each season

Love has its own rationale, it stoops not to reason
So better if people would an insane call me
What others may whisper, I hear and see
I am myself responsible for each of my joy
If I find it in love, none can ask me as why?
I know all the scenes, but these couldn't have been
Ever part of my life that is filled with vain strife
Yet, I look at each throng as if it is for me
And listen to each song as if it is for me
I know you can't love me, as I may not be up
To the mark you deserve or that you visualise
Despite each disparity and each differentiation
I keep myself glued to the sweetness of passions
That I have for you
I would crave for you
I would yearn for you, I will burn for you
And nothing else than love can I earn for you
For love is my sustenance, love is my existence
Love is unbridled flow that yields not to resistance
Love is my palace and a place of repose
Love is my earthen lamp that silently glows
When I fill it with feelings and calm, unseen tears
I am a solitary song that nobody would hear
And you too wouldn't mind as to what is around
That unaccompanied person whose sad songs resound
From sharp edge of a cliff and a yellowed fallen leaf
Anyway, I can't leave you, for life is brief
How sweet would it be if you too could love me
But this is a dream that I so often see

Dream is my theme for I relish in dreams
When realities are far off, I would hug silly whims
And the loveliest whim is that sometime you
would smilingly tell me that I love you too.

©Younas Rehman

-36-

I Am Not A Poet, I Just Yell Aloud

Perhaps just for nothing has someone
Got annoyed with me with no thought
As to what is haunting my unfortunate lot
I too am a human being and an angel not
And this adds to an already accumulated heap
Of my sorrows, agonies and regrets deep
Yet I will give things a second thought
For I am obligated to retain and keep
Intact the ties that we both have had
Invested time and spirit of emotions
To keep the yacht of attachment in motion
My beloved, I didn't forget you ever
I keep you remembered in each segment of time
I am not a poet, I just yell aloud
As if nobody in the vast scattered crowd
Can notice ever what I wish to be heard
Thus filled with blood is my every word
My love, if ever possible it had been
I would have flown to the land where you
Fill with fragrance each colour and hue

As to how I love you, that I know well
For words and narratives would always fail
To depict the picture of the deepest fathoms
Of oceans where feelings of attachment dwell.

©Younas Rehman

-37-

Get Inside Yourself That Needs You Badly

Forget and put aside those selfish lot
Who come into your life as a loss and they
In the sunshine of chances make their hay
Forgetting all that you did for them
Desert them who have deserted you
Your life depends not on who is who
Of them are some who are just venom
Their apathy agonises the depths of the soul
And embittering moments of your life whole
Break those oaths, whose observance breaks you
And for whom you pledged them, acknowledge these not
Turn not your life into fragments of thought
That isn't anything else than delusion
Welcome a safe, comforting seclusion
Leave those orchards that fill your palm
With pointed, sharp, thorns of harm
If dust is the destiny of a fruitless journey
Abandon such pathways that exhaust you only
Get inside yourself that needs you badly
Stop listening to songs that turn you sadly

It is that inner core of your very being
That deserves priority above each other thing
For none else but 'yourself', self, it is
That tries each moment to see you pleased
And let me tell you that strange are the ways
And lands of love that allure each eye
Blind to the fact that where flowers bloom
All around them, poignant thorns lie
Love turns unilateral as beloved deserts
A time comes up when each memory hurts
Ambitions may turn into heaps of sorrow
Devouring each vanity of aimless tomorrow
Waste not your time nor fill it with woes
The brook of time so irrevocably flows
It would care never for these or those
Having nothing to do with who comes in or goes
Then learn from the traits of time your gait
Bury unpaid for passions in the debris of fate
And draw new lines of luck on your palms
Grow new plants in the newly found farms
Love only those souls who would love you as well
Or else, you be ready to mourn and yell
With desperate cries below the blue skies
And watching how eventually a pained passion dies.

©Younas Rehman

-38-

Let It Be Deferred Until Sometime Next

Which agonies shattered the sprite of my craving
Which things lost me the solace that I pined for having
Who has broken this citadel of delicate passions
Who has darkened this heart where nestled sensations
Of love and desire that I used to admire
I can't tell it right now as I feel much perplexed
Let it be deferred until sometime next

And you my beloved should insist on it not
That I should make public each feeling and thought
Some feelings just raw, some emotions refined
Some yearnings got fulfilled while some were declined
These can't be spoken by voice or text
Let it be deferred until sometime next

I own my weaknesses and the constraints around
I know as to why real love was not found
You weren't disloyal neither I could be so
But, watch how the dark brooks of sad times flow
The wounded desires that eventually died

Their dead bodies need not again resurrect
Let it be deferred until sometime next

The world is a playground and each soul a player
In this game of passions perhaps each thing is fair
Who won and who lost builds a separate story
Regardless of that we may put in our share
In this limitless game of riddles and facts
Let it be deferred until sometime next.

-39-

Dwindling Smile

The youthful days came, lasted for a while
And then parted away with a dwindling smile
That colourful period of tones and tunes
Those notes of music that made life Royal
Went and parted away for good
At times, like a stranded stranger
I look back through casements of my own memory
The beauty of the bygone youthful glory
And recall the moments of early romance
That made my soul and passions dance
In some mortal's love
The wine is there in front of me still
But can bring me no more that thrill
That youth could squeeze out of the same
I came not here with my own sweet will
I was created and made to come
God created and detached me from His own being
Like other things, I too remained a thing
God knows to whom was I entrusted
And now bids me adieu the world I trusted
And I got consumed, exhausted and rusted

Through the disconnect between God and His creatures
I know that sands of time are gone
With no grains ahead for me to tread on
Yet my thoughts are so stuck in the past
Blind to the fact that past time is lost
Before saying adieu to the world where I live
I see that await me ahead times new
A grand eternity that knows no end
No grief, no regrets, no loss, no pains
As the boat I voyage in is sailing ahead
And is carrying me to the very stead
Where I will confront the one who made
And sent me here for a small respite
I shall meet God of mercy and might
Getting relieved of all I suffered
And pains of wishes that were not realised.

-40-

Eventually

Eventually
I had to see this agonised day
I can't defog the misty ambience around
Even my very self cannot be found
To a far-off, distant soul I remain bound
Losing my identity
By the way, it isn't my first love
I have loved perhaps countless times
Each love was born and then dwindled away
But this time, its grip is too deep
Distance and disappointment persistently creep
Into my heart, the permanent seat of love
Where passions burn to create heat of love

I know, those days of youthful phase are gone
The colours look faded and the body feels degraded
But the soul is still an undiminished complete whole
And I see that I need to cherish passions whatsoever
And maintain attachments and relations whatsoever
For life would look much more miserable if
I behave like a lifeless yellowed fallen leaf

Even sadness is not a badness, for a feeling it is
Storms are also welcome if I lose a gentle breeze

My love, I know some memories, some past recollections
Related to you are not without dejection
But that all is alright, for fate executes its rules
Who am I to decide the course of connection
Tides of time and strides of destiny
Are constant companions of the relational journey
I won't repeat what has been hurting me
You can for yourself all these things see
The only thing that I say is a sigh
A wordless message, a soundless cry
These are the moments that defy escape
I am entrapped in an exit less trap

At times, I think I should not have loved
But that is just an idea unfounded
It isn't done, it is never grounded
In the human optional domain of desire
But alternatively, if it could be so
Again I would my passions to glow
With the heat of gentle flameless fire
What makes me live is the strength of desire.

-41-

Some Tales

Some tales are fated
To remain just tales
Unheard cries, unnoticed yells
Some tales are meant to remain incomplete
In the book of life that's so much replete
With other highly accomplished stories
Some tales can't see their glamours and glories
We keep on reading these endless tales
And feel as treading on bendless lanes
Perhaps these incomplete stories are meant
To give our life some new dimension
Which probably we could some next time mention
And this vain desire remains haunting our mind
Instead of front line, we keep looking behind
Oh that we could part with desire
Of someone's remembrance, whom we can't acquire

This is our life filled with episodes
Some meant to regret, some to admire.

©Younas Rehman

-42-

Beggar Unknown

Life was given to me as a penny thrown
In charity to some beggar unknown
Neither I could be a luminary star
Nor any glamour could I ever own
Neither an artist could I ever be
Nor could I attract someone's sweet tone
I could not be a light ray for someone's eye
I remained within myself as a smouldering moan
I might have been gifted with some potentials
Getting no chance to be unveiled and shown
I live in loneliness even amidst friends
I came, I am living, and will leave alone

©Younas Rehman

-43-

And That Is Just You.

O, the strangeness of mine, my being found nowhere
In a weird existence where I am not known
I keep on pursuing my recognition elsewhere
Whatever I may be, I need some milieu
And that is just you

I think I am estranged from my wishes as well
Still, one desire keeps me closed in a shell
That desire besides hurting is gladdening too
And that is just you

People come up and leave with all new times
And I too am being drained to unforeseen climes
But my glance remains fixed just on one hue
And that is just you

My loneliness is much agonising for me
But glad, while lonely, you too cannot be

For one soul the meaning of life is true
And that is just you.

-44-

I Could Not Be Stable As I Was Not Able

Is this a wine house, or a glass of wine
That has inebriated all senses of mine
Or this is an entire world in itself
That blends my injured words in a yelling line
A world of feelings and saddened emotions
A place of get together for my straying notions
It is my heart that constantly changes
The spectrums and vintages along the ranges
Of my own reflections and my unbridled thought
My pleasures, my agonies, my yearning lot
With whom to fight, against whom to complain
When I have myself chosen a den
For living alone and brooding on whims
And laughing like insane on a lonely lane
Yea! All these sprout from within my heart
These are just jumbles, and no piece of art
I am not a poet, rather I have been
A dead straw blown off by blowing winds
At times I find myself inebriated
And at moments other, I feel much elated

I could not be stable, as I wasn't able
To know myself or earn a label
Of being someone else than what I am
I am still wondering as to why I came
Into a world which was never a place
To grant me even a bit of grace
Anyhow, I have no other alternative
Than to accept an aimless existence
Where on each step I meet some resistance
But this gloomy picture isn't a whole
Story of my feelings, body and soul
There might be some purpose in mind of God
To grant me a life that is seemingly odd
For the very heart that has been granted to me
Might be "a would be source " of glee
When it finds in itself a flame of love
For the One who creates and stands above
All that we feel, be it woe or thrill
For life is a voyage, a journey uphill
To reach the stars where souls are to find
The final destination that is predestined.

©Younas Rehman

-45-

The Universe As It Is Stays Obscure

Eventually I peeped into my very being
And found that almost everything
Is linked with what my ego reflects
Be these vanities or solid facts
The universe, as it is, stays obscure
And I feel it as my vision recollects
Yea!, The inner being of ours displays
Itself as a world filled with rays
That create universes of colours and thrills
Where flowers do grow atop far-off hills
And valleys that lie beneath our steps
Where structures of nature accord to the maps
That we ourselves draw, be them fair or raw
And all things get reshaped as we heard of, or saw
It is heart where starts every movement and motion
Heart is the citadel of every commotion
Be it an agony or pleasing emotion.

-46-

At Last It Is Heart And Not A Stone

Afflict it not with so many bans
For it may succumb to excessive pains
At last, it is heart and not a stone
Tread it not on such thorny lanes
And why are you angry with the world entire
There may be many, whom you must admire
There may be persons, who really can
Extend true love, if you just remain
Loyal to, and relying on them
Even when you feel no thrill in life
Let your heart play with its vibes
The way it likes instead of being forced
To tune itself with what wit has endorsed
For wit and wisdom have different domain
Than what your feelings may entertain
Imprison it not with polished impressions
For heart is a citadel of candid passions

Let it say what it likes to say
And let it play, as it likes to play.

©Younas Rehman

-47-

Love

Love it is
That either gets related
To whom you are acquainted
Or even to dreams
Which may show you demented
And Life remains ever thirsty for love
Love may be had there
For unknown lands too
Or for orchards that never
Showed you their hue
And beyond it
Love may be for times
That passed and became
Just bygone stories
And yet you are thrilled
By their sweet memories
And at times Love might
Ignite your passions

For building relations
Even with those
For whom you are never
A possible match
A far-fetched pursuit
That reason not suits
But love can also launch
Itself on a branch
Of some tree of paradise
Where morning's sun rises
With heart healing rays
And brighten your days
With unsurpassed beauty
Love can also assume
Itself
As a venomous perfume
That feels pleasing, but
Its thrill tends to kill
It may turn in future
Into hot blazing flames
Of hostility's games
Where passions overrule
Each reason to stay cool
And expectations work
As irreplaceable tool
What may be love's forms
What may be its norms
Whatever regrets

Or credits it may bring
Humanity will always
Continue to sing
Sweetest love songs.

-48-

Accompany Me

Accompany Me
I am an earthly mortal, if accepted, accompany me
If you can go for one by the world rejected, accompany me
I heeded to each one, yet no one cared for me
If you can accommodate a soul neglected, accompany me
My lamp is earthen, and can get blown off anytime
I own no lit up, brightly shining paradigm
Yet as a soulmate you reacted, accompany me
In a dark orchard, luck brought me somewhere
No source for lighting it, I came across here
And being driven to extremity, I had to burn
My own garden, in order some light to earn
If still you appreciate what I have acted, accompany me
My cremated passions, that died long ago
Got reborn once more with a vibrant glow
Kiss these vibes resurrected, accompany me
An ordinary person, with nothing mesmerising

On my own humble stairs, I am steadily rising
If things of these humble origin can stay
As being worth selected, accompany me.

©Younas Rehman

-49-

Yea! Life So Weird, So Shy Of Itself

As the candle got lit, the moths awakened
Scripts and signatures of gone by past
Came forward as images being carved afresh
The story of getting awakened goes on
Griefs and agonies of journeys at hand
Still wrap the tracts of life's sands
This is however never a response alone
To passions, reactions and feelings I own
Many physical factors, many segments material
Of what build a life did borrow a loan
From destiny that so far has been haunting me
At each step some agony accompanied each glee
Yea! Life so weird, so shy of itself
I had willy nilly to receive and lead
Compatible not to what I do or I did
Procrastination, silent storms of passion

Did away with imageries that could build a relation
Of mine with life and with events around
That might someway adorn with eventual love's goal
The dreams I had dreamt during this life whole.

©Younas Rehman

-50-

I Lost Countless Dreams

I lost countless dreams that had once fascinated
My imagery, my feelings and my sweet recollections
Now time appears to have turned its side
After having slept idly and wishing to hide
The annals of past from the eyes of present
As if these no more appear as pleasant
You too are now yearning for some new relation
I too stand obliged to some new fit of passion
Though still I can't really think and believe
As to how things could form a countenance new
I gaze at the new horizons of time
That passes so swiftly and silently tell
Some incomplete stories in rhythm and rhyme
Some annals of gone by segments of past
Though all things look changed and scenario looks different
I still feel the flavour and fragrance that once
Had drawn me and drained me in a stream of romance
And that you of you still remains within me
Whatsoever you're now and wherever you be
For vibes of love never thoroughly wither
They splash back somewhere, either hither or thither

This being what I feel makes me think of the past
Of things that were got and of things that were lost
Life is bargain of losses and gains
Much too has been seen and much too remains.

©Younas Rehman

-51-

Anyway, By The Way, Human I Am

Oh that on this land someone had been there
Who could appreciate the state of my feelings
To whom I could tell what goes on here
Who could know my whispering tales of agony
Who could feel the weight of steps I take
While treading alone on my helpless journey
I urge for someone as a loyal friend
Who would stand by me on each turn and bend
On the ever bending road of existence
I still have vibes that I had someone
Who could wipe my tears that well up in my eyes
Who bring me round when I get morose
And when I fall, they would help me rise
I know it is world, not a bed of roses
Here thorns grow too, it can't be paradise
I am not a landlord, nor an influential too
I am not adorned with a shining hue
Neither I could ever be a man of art
Nor I could win someone's mind and heart
Anyway, by the way, human I am

Claiming never for a high flown glamour or fame
A simple and sincere soul there should be
To understand me and stand by me
In hours of agony and sprites of glee.

©Younas Rehman

-52-

Regrets Galore

Enough you stood with, enough you bore
And you found nothing, save regrets galore
Afraid of losing? You lost so much already
Afraid of being a persona ungratis
You are already that one,
To love you no-one is ready
Does sanity tell you to be inebriated
Does wisdom motivate to remain gyrated
Around the rivet of silencing hinge
All this are bunkum that humility brings
Get your sword and slay your timidity.

©Younas Rehman

-53-

You Ask Me

You ask me as to how much love I had
For the one whom I have always held
As my beloved, and had never failed

In celebrating all the norms of love
I can't tell as to how much, but I do affirm
My love is strong enough and fairly firm

To withhold the breakage of my body and nerves
And the loving heart always retains and conserves
The love that my soul for your soul observes
The chambers of my heart your soul reserves

I am an ordinary man on this earth
And I can't boast of extra ordinary birth
I am made of clay, my beautiful belle
And all my weaknesses I frankly tell

Yet the warmth, charm and spell
Of your attachment will turn not frail

They will hold their sway on each way I tread
Till I am no more when I am dead

And even when I am resurrected again
I would be voyaging on the same love's lane
Which I had been doing during life's span
That I had on this earth for you before
So love won't ever see the word "no more"

Love everywhere, and love galore
If only your soul could as well explore
My heart will be knocking at your door

You are my moon that glows in full bloom
Suspicion of failure has got no room
In the paper meant to examine love
Love transcends each thing, love stands above

The barriers and obstacles of time and space
Love has its own world of glory and grace
Let's be hopeful that at some turn of fate
We would be uniting and would celebrate

The jubilation of unending relation
An unceasing love and an undying passion.

-54-

My Belle

My belle, I knew well that you too would one day
Get dazzled
By vanity of your glamorous beauty
And the unmatched placement that you occupy

But true was the fear that had caught my eye
It did happen so
That I enjoy no more
The welcoming gesture
That I received before

I knew, I knew
My sweetheart I knew
That things will eventually get hues new
Better enjoy the end of this game
I have no regrets and reserve no claim

Leave me, desert me, neglect and ignore me
Who said that come with a love's pledge before me

You did a right job, you split and tore me
And scattered relentlessly my torn off pieces

But I gathered them all to compose myself again
Without a shred of agony or strain
I got born anew and embraced new hue
Like a shining silvery drop of dew

I shone on the petals of my own aspiration
That got resurrected
After sacred cremation
And now I am bidding you congratulation

Stay blessed and happy wherever you be
Somewhere, somehow shall I too find glee
As someone, somewhere there might be
Relegate me my old love! to the chilliest oblivion
I will peacefully stay where I have been driven

I must not be given the slightest compassion
Bye bye to the slaughtered and butchered relation
On destiny's road it was perhaps a good bend
A Point beyond which we could no more lend

Passionate unity and warmth of amity
We were perhaps to part with a much broken heart
Or else it was destiny's sad piece of art

But before we part and say
God be with you
Please see

As to how the cremated old passions
Could eventually usher in a sigh of relief
When it brings an end to our story of grief.

©Younas Rehman

-55-

Keep Your Hands Bound In Pure Relation

When glance gets polluted with seeing things wrong
Wash your eyes with tears of repentance
And when your head is raised up in revolt
Teach it an inebriation in humble prostration
And keep your hands bound in pure relation
During your prayer in the Lord's adoration
To keep them prevented from making mischief
Fear no loss, no agony, no grief
And to shun idle talks or injurious phrase
Keep your tongue indulged in God's praise
Stand calm, bow humbly and place your forehead
On ground in order to enable your soul
To access through prostration your Lord Almighty
For it is not majesty but humbleness pure
That heals, that grants, that blesses, that cures
The agonies of spirit and illness of soul
Which isn't your part, but that's your whole
This is existence, this is life's essence
This is search for life, this is magnificence
O, poor and weak spirit! You're not a lump of clay

Just transformed into one biological species
You're to get from your greatest Creator
A being far beyond your own imagination
Just pray, ask for blessings in pure supplication
And get all amenities on scale of infinity
That's the secret of bonds with divinity.

-56-

Love Is The Essence Of Everything

Love it is that introduces to you
Your very inner self inside you
And love it is that grants its hue
To the very essence of who is who
Be it a forest, a woodland or a cottage
Or a settled busy strip of a town
Wherever you live, only love will give
A fully bloomed phase to your identity
Love keeps recognised your very entity
Love sheds its fragrance in each coming season
Love stands for itself its solid reason
Without love, all things would appear just banal
As all scenes derive their charm from the annals
Of love and passion, an enduring relation
Love adds flavour and fervour to each event of life
To each tiring struggle and agonising strife
See the water that falls from high waterfalls
The stream of falling water that nicely calls
Your attention and tells you that
Love it is that you must celebrate

If you get a chance to see the dance
Of dancing birds in awesome romance
You will notice a rhythm and lay of songs
That speak that each joy to love belongs
Behold the cold snow that melts and flows
It gains from sunlight a heat of love
Like a cool shade love smoothly acts
And reveals to our souls solacing facts
When the heated sands of deserts unknown
Scorch our feet, love cools and owns
Our scared hearts and worn up minds
And tells "one who seeks, eventually finds"
And whenever we travel to a far off village
The care that our acquaintances and friends
So passionately and warmly to us extend
This scene of relation, this glow of affection
Speaks loudly that love builds connection
Love must be adored as a sacred statue
Placed in a temple of sacred passions
For love it is that heals the ailing souls
And love it is that builds relations
Yet love at the same time is delicate too
With its breakage it can break down you
Let the idol of love fall not or else
It can ruin all of life's lovely tales
And injure your soul like pointed pieces
Of a broken, shattered and scattered glass
Love can also bring agonies, woes and pains
It can fling you into the darkest dens
Of chilliest despair, where no one hears
The moans and sighs of a broken soul

The dewy evenings and the glazing days
Borrow their charms from the glowing rays
Of dreams that we dream in our lonely nights
When memories stir up and show their light
Love is a rain and love is a snow
And love it is that appears as glow
Of shining dew drops on leaves of crops
Love is your victory and your defeat
It makes you either advance or retreat
Love is the presence of your very being
Love is the essence of everything.

©Younas Rehman

-57-

How Long?

How long
Would you be obsessed with suppressing the fiction
Of your limitless longing, unquenchable addiction
For having your untold yearnings accomplished
Are you scared of notoriety? You are already steeped
Deep in the dark dens of social disapproval
You need not make a fuss about your inner upheaval
And go on longing for what doesn't belong
To you anymore
My heart, if you think of quitting your desire
Just for the reason that none will admire
Your whimsies and vanities
Then tell me what the plainest realities do
Each fact is subjective, all reasons accrue
To build up a huge, unfathomable whim
You may for the time being feel satisfied
That you've quitted desires that were not realized
But how is that possible?
Except left alone, nothing else would you own
The orchards of longings by now have grown
Into woodlands of dreams and inseparable themes

A limitless array of innumerable beams.
Now the session of owning or disowning is over
Do what you can, you can't stop being a lover
Now, love is departure and love is arrival
From the soil of love sprouts your survival
No question, no answer, no query again
This game will not end with tormenting your brain
With making accounts of losses or gains
All that was probable has already occurred
Just go on with all that is going on now
And assess not the merits and demerits of love.

©Younas Rehman

-58-

Inconsistency Is Baffling My Mind

I live, I see, I think just to find
That Inconsistency is baffling my mind
Either I am a mismatch or the world may be so
The world couldn't know me, nor could I ever know
As to what the world is with its so many rifts
Affluence, poverty, and numerous sifts
That segregates us into so many segments
And tears us apart into countless fragments
Is it time or just our split attitudes
Each time our agonising thoughts get renewed
The age demands one thing and logic the other
Changes suggest one thing and desire another
Inconsistency looms bigger around
For which of my longings can I find a ground
When groundless appears each wish, each desire
But warm expectations still linger on there
Perhaps a spark would ever burst into fire
To give me eventually some beams of light
In the wee hours of the long suffered night
This too is a dream and that too is a dream

Effort is vanity and fate too is a dream
Depth is illusory and so is the height
Nothing is permanent, each phase is ephemeral
Your glitter is transient, my gaze is ephemeral
And this very thought has been the only source
Of soothing my pains, though not of delight.

-59-

And He Took It

I got dissolved
And he took it for my full extinction
Knowing not that
I would still carry my distinction
In one or another tinge
I kept mum
And he deemed that
Now things are done
But instead
My voice became widespread
All that he could
Was that no longer I would
Remember him
So what
He could not be the only theme
To cover the whole
The span of my life
Let me now come
To my very self
Let me open up
The closed-down shelf

Of my own heart
But I am never
Only a heart
Body, brain, mind and limbs
Each one is a significant part
Of my whole existence
And so on passions
Rests not persistence
I have to go through
Numerous toils
And travel onward
For many many miles
To eventually reach
Some safe coastlines
After having voyaged
Through the long-stretched sea
Of odds and obstacles
And loads of pledges and obligations
And once ashore
I will knock at the door
Of some complacent soul
Who won't wait for a luminary
And accept just an ordinary
Chap like me.

-60-

Oh That Someone

Oh that someone on this land had been there
Who could appreciate the state of my feelings
To whom I may tell what is going on here
Who could know the whispers of my agonised feelings
Who could feel the weight of the steps I take
While treading alone on some deserted track
I urge for someone as a loyal friend
Who would stand by me on each turn and bend
On the ever-bending pathway of existence
I still have vibes that I should have had
A loyal companion who would bring me round
When I at times would go morose
Who could wipe my tears that well up in my eyes
Who brings me around when I get morose
And whenever I fall, they would help me rise
I know that life can't be a bed of roses
Things aren't the way that desire proposes
I never long for a lofty heaven
I only wish that I may be given
A simple, sincere and caring friend

Who would stand by me on each turn and bend
Of this hilly road of ephemeral existence
And who would withstand the severity of seasons
Where feelings override the heights of reasons.

©Younas Rehman

-61-

Am I Nothing But A Weird Tale Only?

Am I nothing but a weird tale only?
Bulldozed at daylight and reconstructed
During the late hours of the night when
Passage of light rays is obstructed
Or else that is a dream, an illusioned sensation
Solacing my heart with its inebriation
I carried on writing and saw at the end
The paper I wrote over was blank as before
Perhaps the words that were written fortuitously
Carried no meaning and sense any more
Perhaps something mysterious is there in nature
Each petal is bearing an unknown signature
Some linkage appears in time and distance
The neighbouring space shows a marked curvature
Apart from this spectacle of background factors

I wish I could find a simpler correlation
Between pride of beauty and the warmth of passion.

©Younas Rehman

-62-

The Way That Lies

The way that lies between two souls
One has to consume a good deal of time
And a pain that travels to someone else
Needs some wounds to feel the same
One has to be tolerant to feel the feelings
Of those whose pains are not revealing
But as for the call across the wall
Of blurred rendition of my passions all,
I can't assign a princely position
To annals of heart, whether gladdening or sad
It is not a question of good or bad
I yell aloud, if only I had
A good opportunity for quenching the thirst
Of hidden desires that tend to burst
I would have done all that I could
I know at times I have to remain
Silent and calm, though I equally can
Speak to the walls
if I wish to speak all
Things that impact me

That is so easy, as
They will not reject me
But still a taciturn
I tend to remain.

©Younas Rehman

-63-

My Heart Was Broken By Your Words Too

Though I can't ascribe; each bad luck to you
For many other events that happened to me
Had also their hand in building this milieu
My hopes and ambitions were vain and futile
My psychology was likewise also fragile
Saddening were things that I had to pursue
But my heart was broken by your words too

I hoped that rainfall might shower some wine
To fill with a romance my life's timeline
This was a dream that I had to pursue
But my heart was broken by your words too

I am not a pessimist nor do I carp any season
I own that existence has meaning and reason
That unfolds itself in a pleasurable hue
But my heart was broken by your words too

I had to take care of my social obligations
And show wholesome fealty for chains of traditions

Suppressing each thought in the den of inhibition
In the heart's slaughterhouse with my own hands
I had to throttle each living and throbbing ambition
So much I cared for each social taboo
But my heart was broken by your words too

They are mine and they won't cease to belong
To me, this remained the theme of my song
But realities exposed that my ideas were wrong
Eventually failed tales of beauty and beau
My heart was broken by your words too.

©Younas Rehman

-64-

O, My Life!

O, my life!
I didn't tell them anything about you
Anyway, they have guessed all things through
Seeing a dwindling glow in my painful eyes
Though I kept hidden my loud yet unheard cries
And as for your care, I said nothing to them
As an unknown stranger, I slyly came
And took my way to a forlorn land
Where I have no acquaintance, nor a close by friend
Yet they read you through the words I penned
Adamant in keeping my vibes hidden till end
So far, from all of them I have remained
Though in this trade of love, nothing I gained
Yet, like fragrance, it could not remain veiled
And spreading all around, it had to get spelled
And I found that love's vibes cannot be concealed
Anyhow, anyway, it is finally revealed
As matter is out, and that secret is no more
A secret, I am feeling compelled to adore
You just openly, whether you acknowledge it or not
For love depends not on a futile thought

Of its being recognised, or even regretted
Love will go on, on its own, without being caught
In a cage of dependence or mesh of relevancy
My sweetheart, I won't beg you for any clemency
I am myself love, and love is my existence
Despite all the obstacles and bitter resistance

-65-

I Loved You Like My Life

I loved you like my life and you
Saw me as if a stranger was I
You can forget, disown and deny
Whatever you think to be better for you
But as for me, I'm used to pursuing
That very fragrance, colour and hue
That makes me only think of you
Perhaps neither you nor I could think
That my very being would eventually sink
In the sea of tears and dens of sorrow
This was what I was fated to borrow
And now when all things seem to have been
Changed completely and encapsulated
By vagaries, whims and wants outdated
I remain all the same absorbed in thought
That what should be chased and what should be not
We both were initially treading the same
Track of belongingness and fealty though
Who could know what the sunset would show
You shined as the moon while I had to swoon
In the darkness around where nothing is found

Else than a cry that would nobody hear
And a life condensed in a droplet of tear
But such things happen in this game of belonging
One is crowned with pride, the other burning in longing
Yet I don't mean that I have regrets
Over anything which a true passion begets.

-66-

Yet I Am Understood To Be Someone

Yet I am understood to be someone
Who is just a barrier along some way
Though I have nothing to do with others
And pass lonely my night and day

Yet I am understood to be someone
Who might be inclined in this world to none
Though I am impressed and infatuated
By thousands of nature's pure gems
I've done all things that could be done

Yet I am understood to be someone
Worth not the salt of time's flow
Standing unseen in a jam-packed row
I used to glow when I had my day
I stayed everywhere where I could stay
All the same people are prone to say
That I deliberately missed each chance

To see my destiny bloom and dance
In a glamorous display of romance
And I am understood to be someone
Nothing worthwhile who has ever done.

©Younas Rehman

-67-

And That Is Just You

O, the strangeness of mine, my being found nowhere
In a weird existence where I'm not known
I keep on pursuing my recognition elsewhere
whatever I may be, I need some milieu
And that is just you
I think I am estranged from my wishes as well
Still, one desire keeps me closed in a shell
That desire besides hurting is gladdening too
And that is just you
People come up and leave with all new times
And I too am being drained to unforeseen climes
But my glance remains fixed just on one hue
And that is just you
My loneliness is much agonising for me
But glad, while lonely, you too can not be
For one soul the meaning of life is true
And that is just you.

©Younas Rehman

-68-

Mirage

In this space time continuum where time is merged
And runs like blood in the arteries of space
Lie many a question you can never address
In this world of deceits, God can never be found
As darkness of obscurity always surround
A mind that tries to find its Creator
They say that seeing is believing and as such
An idea of unseen God seems weird so much
But things that have already been seen
Understood fully these too haven't been
You can try as well many mirrors of knowledge
You can try instruments that people acknowledge
And likewise, you may make big sacrifice
But to find your God, nothing will suffice
From most adamant atheist to most orthodox believer
From ordinary person to most luminary viewer
All have their logic of equivalent appeal
And as such Faith has been very complex a deal
This world is a wonderland of mirages galore
Save fantasy you can nothing else explore
In this world of ours all whims are equivalent

All distractions are same and all dreams are equivalent
The world is a mirage, each its sight is a mirage
Here day is a mirage, also night is mirage
But who said you failed, seeing not God around
It is none of your business to have God found
Your job is just seek Him rather than leak Him
Down in bits of wit you can't ever break Him
You're just a sportsperson and go on to play
Carry on playing till the end of this day
You are a player and this world a playground
Here nothing is lost, here nothing is found
Play and just play on the role for this day
Remember you have been a small bit of clay
And you are going through process of getting transformed
Into being that could by then get well informed
Of all things remaining in this world obscure
Just wait as in patience lies all your cure
Think neither of victory nor anything else
Who plays his role wins and who thinks of it fails
For this very playground is meant just for playing
And thinking is only a tool of delaying
This day shall be over and when new Sun rises
The next day is meant for awarding the prizes
And then shall you see your God with your eyes.

-69-

I Am Awfully Scattered

I am awfully scattered to the extent that
Nothing appears to compose me again
Even an angelic touch of yours
Can't heal the wounds that my lot entertains
My feet are fettered, l wish someone came
To release me free and unlock the same
On my "live life", I've wept a lot
And no tear is left to shed on its corpse
That fervour is gone and that zeal is no more
All flowers got withered, I see thorns galore
My poetry is blank, it deserves no rank
No rhythm, no rhyme, no idea to bank
In lines called fine, as I am confined
In haphazard array I get my words lined
The pain isn't that on someone depends
The joys and pleasures of my own life's sands
The pain is that person could not be my own
Remaining indifferent to love that was sown
On soil of soul where love had been grown
For someone who always remained someone else

Who condescends not to value my tales
Impervious to response of heart-rending yells
My jewels of passions adorning my soul
Were treated as valueless pieces of coal.

©Younas Rehman

-70-

Wonder Not

Wonder not as to what it is
The feel of a cool mysterious breeze
Creeping deep in your heart's recesses
You hear a sound, that gently caresses
The soul, either inside or around you
A distant dream that has found you
Someone is there who hasn't seen
Your face and yet he has always been
Remembering you, the way as though
You've been with him since long ago
My unheard song reaches you somehow
You can hear my heartbeats resound with love
Since both of us are reluctant so far
To openly say as to what things are
That run and go between both of us
The vibes that flow between both of us
So go the annals of love unsettled
And a stable relation didn't grow between us
A ray of hope is still there ahead

That this siege of thorns will turn at last
Into flowery bed of happy romance
If life gave us again a good chance.

©Younas Rehman

-71-

The Flowers Of Our Relationship's Garden

The flowers of our relationship's garden
Await being watered with a lovely smile
Or else, they would wither away
If you couldn't come and stay
Just for a while
Each of my heartbeats
Entreats
Your sweet self
To come
And you would have to see
Me
For the sake of love
That we owe to each other
I see a tinge of breaking relation
I feel my hopes are going to collapse
With the lapse
Of time
Some norms and some social codes are there
Or regard for someone's words is to bear
Anyway

Probably our intimacy won't stay
Yet a ray of hope shines there
Glimmering in my broken heart
That you won't let me go forlorn
You won't like to leave me alone
On my hope's behest
I request
Your sweet self
To come and save me
From being deserted
For the world it maybe
Just an ordinary event
But getting broken of a loving heart
Is not a commonplace piece of art
In the game of love
It is rather complete ruination
Of life, of love, of sweet relation
The gatherings, the unions and meetings together
All would get devoid of hue
If you
Didn't take care
Of a languishing soul
Hope you will accede
To my entreaties
To save entities
Of love relations
And yearning passions
Hope you won't like
Tears in my eyes
Hope you will give
Me a pleasant surprise

Of seeing me and solacing me
Of hugging me and embracing me
To save my hopes
From obliteration
In separation
But hazards and sad apprehension
Also, rise
In my tearful eyes
That trusting in my sweet illusions
May prove unwise
And our relation
Might not be able
To keep me stable
My love, do come
For the sake of love
That blend of two souls
In sweetest ties
Dry my eyes
With your soothing palm
And on my wounds
Rub the balm
Of lovely smile
I had a vanity
A trusted pride
That you would abide
With words of love
This pride seems to getting smashed
And the vision of beauty seems to have crashed
With arrogant pride
But yet a ray of hope exists
Which resists

My despair
As it is a question of life
Of the age-long relation
So, no option else than seeing me
Is left with thee
My love, my life, my gem
Do come, do come, do come.

©Younas Rehman

-72-

A Wave Of Craving

A wave of craving and hope combined
Has struck the seashore of my soul and mind
Where my passions and desires reside
Perhaps some new and fresh breeze has blown
Taking my imagery into a world unknown
The seeds of ambitions that I had once sown
Have by now into such big orchards grown.
A thought is perpetually striking my mind
That now it is time to pack and wind
up all such memories that furnish affliction
And old stories by now deserve deletion
Love should be welcomed if it is accepted
And it needs to be equipped if the same is rejected
Ambers of passion should receive a price
And the rays it gives off must be reflected
The bulk of my life span I've already spent
In weaving and sewing up fragmented feelings and ambitions
And pulling along with all forms of restrictions
But no longer ever r I intend to let time

Slay what I find as the rhythm and rhyme
Of song that I sing just to lull my pained tales
I look for a freedom where happiness dwells.

-73-

On Time's Sand

This beauty, this glamour, this youthful glow
All these splendours shall smoothly flow
Into a den destined at its ultimate end
On track of tides on time's sand
Nor my poems will have their lyrics
Nor will the music display its charm
Yet the world will go on blooming
New flowers will keep on sprouting
And new songbirds will be chanting there
With melody and sweet scent everywhere
I will be gone, like a burst of the bubble
And all my contemporary friends as well
Will not be here to laugh or knell
Yet the world will remain populated
With newly sprouted souls and throngs
New mindsets, trends and love-filled songs
Yet I feel happy with all that goes
I feel elated with the time that flows
As though I not, but my inner soul knows

That I'm not here to come and go
Like a streamlet of melted snow.

©Younas Rehman

-74-

I Know It Well

I know it well
That you were meant
To dwell away
From me as well
If you had to part
Then you should have told
At the very start
What tempted thee
To reside inside
That unlucky heart
That had no thought
That you would part
My soul! This tale
Isn't the whole
Story of life
Many a strife
Other than love
Hover above
My lonely existence
Though I know it
And knew it too

That time can turn up
With some new hue
Nonetheless I
Could do nothing more
Than knock at the door
Which would never open
Yet with all this
I still admire
A love that rests
Above all expectations
For love isn't a relation
Of give and take
Love always treads on
It's chosen track
Yet, love after all craves
For getting acknowledged
And wants to hear
A word or two
That I too love you.

©Younas Rehman

-75-

Let There Be

Let there be
Some words
To unveil your being
And a state of mind
Be specified
To expound me
Thoroughly
Let the journey
From you to me
Be chalked out
Through knowing
Both of us
Mutually
I need a mirror
That may show aptly
Your matchless beauty
If it showed you
As you are
It will tend to bring a match
Of beauty
That has no match

And let there be
A discerning eye
To assess your being
And declare you
To be the flag bearer
Of beauty par excellence
I stand and walk
To reach somewhere
In search of fallen
Piece of Heaven
To find a lost paradise
Where someone
Might be there
To take my name
In a friendly vein
I saw and faced
Many an autumn
And gently embraced
The sharpest thorns
Now let someone be
So friendly to me
Who would console
My languished soul
As a barren desert
My heart remained
Bleak and listless
And life appeared
Scorned and disdained
Let someone come
Like the breeze of spring
To paint with greenery

Everything
In my barren heart
In this land of sorrows
Of hopeless tomorrows
I need a today
Which may
Grant me companionship
Of a loving friend
Who would soothe
My long-suffered pains
And turn into flowers
The lonely land
Of my barren Destiny
I need a yell
That may speak aloud
My pent-up passions
And injured emotions
Of deserted relations
I need a yell
To sound the knell
Of my unheard woes
I need a friend
Who knows
My secret glooms.

©Younas Rehman

-76-

Time Passed The Way It Chose

Time passed the way it chose
Events occurred as nature pleased
And I was also part of nature
My existence bore the very signature
As destiny had willed for me
To be servile to
desires unbridled
Was also something
in nature of man
Beauties were planted
and hearts were granted
An eternal thirst
To remain dedicated
To unquenchable thirst.

©Younas Rehman

-77-

A Dream That Aspires

An insatiable thirst
Tends to burst
Me
A thirst that trickles down
To the depth of my soul
And captivates my whole
Being
A dream that aspires
And pines
For its realisation
A fire that ignites
My unbridled passion
For lodging on some dreamlands
Of my sweet imagery
Yes it is love
And in the density of desire
That sets the fire
My whole existence
O, love! for heaven's sake
Tell me at least

Was it the substance and the only gist
Of life
To be aspiring for someone else
Whose fruitless company always fails
To give me a sense
Of satisfaction
Nor whose touch even, heals my passion
Her presence in gatherings does enthral
All
But I find her seeing an imperfect act
Making me only
To pick and collect
The pains I receive
The smiles that deceive
Whether I get access or not
Both my success and failure are fraught
With subsequent yearnings
Saddening heart-burnings
And agonised illusions
My plans and efforts
Are ending in ashes
And the fading flashes
Of my frail expectations
Are a permanent source
Of endless lamentations
Was it that I came
To witness a game
Of mysterious life
Where being and not being

Exhibit equality
Where pride and joy
End in humility
Of cherished hopes.

©Younas Rehman

-78-

When You Come To See Me Now Again

When you come to see me now again
Long after you had seen me by then
You will probably find me having grown older
But to this day even
I do remain
The same ardent lover as ever before
Though sands of time
Have carried me into
A quite new land, weather and clime
Nonetheless, more or less my gaze
Will keep on grazing and chasing the face
That turned me different in different ways
I won't be able to forget you ever
Though bygone past could be retrieved never
But one thing is certain my passionate love
For you would always stay and endure
I am love in myself and love is me
Whatever time and tide would be
Nothing special do I need to think of
I love you because you are simply you

Beyond any question or inquisition
That, what is what and who is who
Maybe when you come up next time
To see me as how I am
I may be only a forgotten tale
I might have gone to from where I came
Yet from the clouds of distant wilderness
You would hear perhaps a yearning yell
That vibes of old love still prevail.

©Younas Rehman

-79-

I Am An Earthen Lamp

I am an earthen lamp
And shall be extinguished
Yeah, I could not win any placement distinguished
An earthen lamp would just die out
As an unheard sigh, I will fly out
I touched all the limits within my ken
And nothing more or greater than
What I did already would be carried on
But something special would perhaps remain
An inaccessible and unfulfilled dream
Someway, somehow I led my life
Pretty or ugly, with regrets or pride
As an open book, I showed them all
Nothing more was left for me to show
And nothing ever I resorted to hide
It was like a night that was meant to end
And you too won't live for good, my friend
Most of the journey of life is done
Whatever time we are left with now
Should be pledged to an endless love
And as a morning we would dawn again

On some distant, unknown, far-off land
Whatever time we are destined to gain
Should be spent with joy as never again
We would be able to live once more
As eventually bangs the closing door.

©Younas Rehman

Collabs

Perhaps

Younas

Dear Belle! Perhaps
The love that I so much cherished
The passions in which I had relished
All of them have grown so dim
As if they are getting perished
My love!
The Intoxication that passion induced
The fervour that my urge produced
All of them seem to have got slumbered
Perhaps their days were numbered

Sunita

Dear Beau! Perhaps
Either me or you have failed to know
That on peaks of life, love has to glow
And echo as well with distant songs
My Beau,
Ever you too felt the hue
With which my soul remains aglow

I too love you and you aren't alone
To lament, cry, scream and moan

Younas

Dear Belle! Perhaps
My soul needed to get relieved
From agonies that it had long cumbered
The sun of earlier craze is setting
I spent my life in futile waiting
And look at the sky with tears in my eye
Asking my destiny as to how and why
This love was meant to see its doom
Amidst the flowers that grow and bloom

Sunita

Dear Beau! Perhaps
I do also own you, as you do me
I too, pine for time of glee
I too so frequently visit the morns
And the sites of sunset, where nights get born
I go through the nights in pain all alone
I too, much pine that you could be my own

Younas

Dear Belle! Perhaps
If all these vibes were just vain vagaries
Memories that could bring nothing else
Than tears and sighs in moaning eyes

What a befitting, grand surprise!
This is how a passion dies
I wish you too could ever visualise
The tears that well up and wet my eyes
Well, my belle! I know it well
You could perhaps never dwell
With me together on the same soil
Where love was born with a single smile

Sunita

Dear Beau! Perhaps
Though much so explicitly it could not be shown
But how could you think that love could ever sink
But why should at last there be a dismay
When both of us can and both of us may
Tell each other as to what goes on
With what has already been decided
By will of God

Younas

Dear Belle! Perhaps
Yet I believe
I might be wrong
Perhaps you too share the song
Of earnest, pure love with me
And possible if only it could be
I will kiss my fate again in glee

Sunita

Dear Beau! Perhaps
If luck could be made and steered
As we would desire
Long ago could have got extinguished
This tormenting distance
And agonising fire
Of being forced to live away from each other
Let's continue our love's sacred journey
And wait for the moment that destiny
Allows us to live together throughout eternity
Just sooth your heart and open your eyes
God from above will bless our love
With wondrous union of being two in one
Let the will of God be done.

Younas Rehman. Karachi, Pakistan
Sunita Grover Raina. Kolkata, India

You Said (Soul Mates)

Sunita

You said
To make me quiet
You will hug me tight
That will end the fight
Shut me up, it might
But who was fighting
I was relaxing

My thoughts enlightening
Confusing your understanding
Your views collapsing

Younas

So it happens, souls connected
They may talk on issues so differently reflected
For mirrors are different on opposite ends
Where rampant stay opposing trends
The talks were reasoned from both sides though
The time needed then a rebirth of glow
That had reunited us long, long ago
So it was not quieting, rather talking again
On things sprung from attachment's grain

Sunita

You said
I always needed to win
But is that a sin
If somehow, crept under your skin
And tell me how, wherein?
But who wants to win
I was discussing a subject
To which you did not object
You tried to wisdom inject
Some explanations I did reject

Younas

Each thing you utter is never denied
For besides your beauty, you've intellect too
Nothing on this earth, whether boundaries or creeds
Can ever separate myself and you
If I won, you won -if you win, I win
For views of both of us have always been
Focussed on same objective and theme
Of love and unity, truth and being fair
But above these all, I have to take care
For the glow of flame that draw us near
That makes two distant souls hold each other dear

Sunita

You said
I should learn to listen
For this is not a competition
Proper reasons with explanation
Should be in every discussion
But who said I was not listening
That I do not speak with reasoning
It was only when you were weakening
That you started sweetening
And then
You said
To make me quiet
You will hug me tight
That will end the fight
Shut me up, it might

Younas

My soul mate, your talks are always sweet
With fragrance of reason and beauty replete
But I also needed to explain such things
From an angle that differs but surely brings
Harmony and oneness and a better cohesion
Between two souls that live in unison
And transcend the gulf of views conflicting
We need a love's bridge when political scenes
Give show of hostility and distancing themes
We are always the winners as long as we remain
True to the spirit of unity and love
For love transcends all barriers and lives above
The things that deter our journey towards
The dreamland of passions where sing the songbirds
Just one anthem, one song of hot passion
So better to hug you and tighten the relation.

Younas Rehman. Karachi, Pakistan
Sunita Grover Raina. Kolkata, India

Pashto Ghazals

Written by Younas Rehman; followed by English translations.

1) دا دے س‌ه رابان‌دے اوکڑل ـ دا دے س‌ه را باندے اوکڑل
اے زما خپل‌ه دلبره ـ دا دے س‌ه را باندے اوکڑل
ن‌ه مے خیال وو ن‌ه مے وہم چه ساتم با ستا یادون‌ه
آ واڑے واڑے خبرے ـ آ اوگده ملاقاتون‌ه
ت‌ه با تلے را تلے جنان‌ه دا انجام ن‌ه بے خبره
اے زما خپل‌ه دلبره۔ دا دے س‌ه را باندے اوکڑل
ن‌ه پ‌ه ما کے س‌ه خوبی وا ن‌ه پ‌ه تا کے س‌ه جادو وا
بس ساده ساده قصے وے۔ هسے عام‌ه گفتگو وا
یو احساس زرغونیدلو۔ رو رو جوړه شوا خبره
سنگ‌ه رو رو لیوانے شووم۔ س‌ه چل اوشو دا زړه سره
اے زما خپل‌ه دلبره۔ دا دے س‌ه را باندے اوکڑل
ارتقا دا یوه احساس وا۔ حادث‌ه ن‌ه وا س‌ه بل‌ه
اؤ بس هسے با را یاد شوے اے آشنا کل‌ه نا کل‌ه
دا واڑو واڑو قصو نا آخر جوړا شوا خبره
اے زما خپل‌ه دلبره‌دا دے س‌ه را باندے اوکڑل
اے زما خپل‌ه دلبره۔ دا دے س‌ه را باندے اوکڑل

I can't unveil as to how this happened
What sorcery did you play my sweetheart
I still remember, we had normal contacts
Common short talks and plain conversations
Marked so frequently our longest sessions
You came and went with no idea at all
That these small things would grow into tall
Trees of attachment and enthralling sensations
Neither I was someone special, nor were you a magician
Simple frivolities grew into a stronger ambition
None of us knew that we weaved a fabric
Of a spellbinding and inebriating magic
A sensation was fated to grow into an orchard
And gradually I

was enamoured
And fell In love with a person
whom I hadn't loved before
Even despite all
her charms Galore
O, the one whom I love!
Can you tell me a bit
As to how I, without you
became incomplete
As for me, things evolved
and events revolved
Around some future that
would turn me dissolved
And subsumed in love
As an eventual destination
of that unthoughtful, plain
And just common relation
I took it for frivolities,
but time had its course
Ordinary weeds were to
grow up as trees
I remembered you then
I remember you now
That was common
Remembering, this
remembrance is love
Would you tell me
my soul mate?
As to what it was

that you did to me
That with you got linked all
my restlessness and glee.

©Younas Rehman

2) کله یو خواهش اؤ کله بل خواهش
ده جوند سره تل تل اوسیگی مل خواهش
کـه ده خوشبو چمن وی
یا ده ارزو وطن وی
که ده جذبو سمندر
په زړه کښ موجزن وی
که ارتقا وی ده سوچ
یا ده عمل خواهش
کله یو خواهش، اؤ کله بل خواهش
بوجھ ده جفا کڑی جوړه
که ده بیلتون ارزو
یا کړی اُمید ده وفا
ده سم تړون ارزو
هر یو بدلون راؤلی، اخپل اخپل خواهش
کله یو خواهش ، اؤ کله بل خواهش
ترخے لمحے ده هجر
خواږے نغمے ده وصل
نا دیده اوښکے ده غم
یا افسانے ده وصل
هر څه په جوند کښ راولی بدل بدل خواهش
کله یو خواهش، اؤ کله بل خواهش
هم ده خواهش نه فرار
ده یو خواهش پخپله
چه څو جوندے وے ارزو
لے زړه بیلیږی کله
ده زندگی ده واڑه ، ده یوه غزل خواهش
کله یو خواهش، اؤ کله بل خواهش

At times one desire
and other times, another desire
Life remains aglow with
flames of yearning's fire
Whether it be an orchard
or a dreamland of passions
Or tumultuous waves
of endless aspirations
Or the evolution of
thought
It ceases not
To be a desire
All the things
eventually spring from
the fountain of desire
The world of romance
is a desire to dance
At times, despair
takes us in a trance
To give up love
But even that emanates
from the fountain of desire
Hopes may get at times
vigour rejuvenated
And we urge for a reunion
with those gone separated
A revival of old bonds
also demands
A sustained desire
Come whatever may
Desires it is

that takes us in
and takes us away
Vary thus things
that we dread or admire
Behind each change
works the hand of desire
Yea, the Love we lend
and the love that we borrow
Wait for a better
solacing tomorrow
And that's as well
a miracle of desire
And desire to quit love
is too a desire
Our life's journey
on destiny's road
Is like a throbbing
vibrant ode
Heard on a shore
of the sea of desires.

©Younas Rehman

Younas Rehman wrote and dedicated this poem to me

A Gem

A gem, a pearl, a sweet bard you are
To shine on the sky of poets as a star
Originally, truth and straightforwardness it is
In your personality that tends to please
Each eye that reads and each ear that hears
Your boldness and fairness welcome no fears
Your passions are pure and transparent ever
To cajoling others you shall bow down never
And as for your beauty, fantastic that is
Your looks produce a soul soothing breeze
And the words that you weave and blend them together
Look like wreathes of gold quills and feathers
An innocent soul with a passionate heart
You are poet an ideal, a person of art
You are adored by whom you're explored
You're neither forgotten, nor ever ignored
By those who appreciate the value of truth
And discern the placement of candidness' fruit.

©Younas Rehman

www.ingramcontent.com/pod-product-compliance
Lightning Source LLC
LaVergne TN
LVHW041210150826
845673LV00001B/348

* 9 7 9 8 8 9 5 5 6 9 9 1 7 *